Protagonists

Protagonists

Nancy Lewis Baenziger

9 P
9 Volcanoes Publishing
Kamuela, HI
Hood River, OR
2022

Copyright 2022 Nancy Lewis Baenziger

Cover and interior design by Nancy Lewis Baenziger

All rights reserved. No part of this book may be reproduced in any manner without written consent of the author/publisher (contact at nlbshort@gmail.com).

Library of Congress CIP data is available.

ISBN: 979-8-9867535-0-8

Disclaimer: This is a work of poetry whose character portrayals represent generalities, reflecting HIPAA privacy practices and a population size large enough to render individual identification impossible. Readers should thus neither draw identity conclusions nor infer that advice is being provided by its words.

9volcanoespublishing.wordpress.com
Kamuela HI 96743
Hood River OR 97031

PRINTED IN THE UNITED STATES OF AMERICA
of which Hawaii is one

Dedication

Insightful wisdom

of Ralph Waldo Emerson

guides my writing's rules

Table of Contents

Observational Studies

    Intrada 3
    Survivors 4
    Covirion 5
    Vigil 6
    Bereft 7
    Bedside Manners 8
    Intensive Care 9
    Front Lines 10
    War Footing 11
    Line in the Sand 12
    Neanderthal 13
    Compline 14
    Consequences 15
    Merge 16
    CovEncore 17

Protagonists

    Common Demon 21
    Hengest 22
    Charismatic 23
    Behind the Counter 24
    Duplex 25
    Duality 26
    Soul Mate 27
    Transmission Lines 28
    October 29
    Carmina Ohana 30
    Table Mannerisms 31
    Colonnade 32

Grandfather 33
Guitarist I 34
Guitarist II 35
Time Capture 36
Hoople ND 37
Harlequin 38
Protagonists 39

Antagonists

Wolf Moon 43
Ghosts 44
Citadel 45
Recipient 46
Semaphoria 47
Ex Cathedra 48
Soft Money 49
Bedeviled 50
Stand-In 51
Suffer Not 52
46XX 53
Prospectus 54
Freak Show 55
Praise Ye 56
Sunrise Service 57
Wiring Diagram 58
Wolf Eyes 59

Border Lines

Jocasta 63
Border Patrol 64
Border Crossing 65

Coda

    Offertory 69
    Standfast 70
    Séance 71
    Mirrored Drives 72
    AfterImage 73
    Poets and Other Crazy People 74
    Territory 75
    Circus Circadius 76
    Retrospective 77
    IndigeDaughter 78
    Standoff 79
    Spectrescopy 80
    Lost Wax 81
    Reframed 82
    Cædmon, sing mē 83

Acknowledgments 85
Selected Explanations 86
About the Author 95

Protagonists

Observational Studies

Intrada

Other sojourners

composite and singular

drift past the mirror

Survivors

Always a smile and a new phrase for each
new face in line at your register day in and day out
your cheerful accent sets apart
each member of the passing procession how many
lines did you live through to have those numbers
written so indelibly on your forearm whose face
do you see in me as I go by?

Christmas carols in the snowy streets cannot muffle
the sounds of passing fire trucks before you sink
to the curb with your hands over your ears
holding inside the scream of air raid sirens
echoing your birth cry even now.

Your voice conversing tightens almost
unnoticed but my eager tongue chattering on about
code-breaking stumbles into shamed
silence before Coventry Cathedral's flames
reflected in your eyes.

Covirion

At first I was but a whisper
coasting on the icy winter wind.
You heard, but you didn't listen.

My friends, while you quarreled I
was waiting with my grinning
death's head hid behind
my hands.

You have dallied far too long
and here I am.

Vigil

Worry has been walking on your face.
      Its footprints show for some time now.

The fingers of fear tighten round
      your throat to catch
      your voice.

How little can we offer but our
      presence in the waiting.

Bereft

Not all that much in the way of close lives lost ...so far .....
        a passed past colleague I knew as a jerk, but still,
knowing now a life lost so far, and it's early.

Previously, at season's end, when summer began,
        while my other broke his
        bow tie's stranglehold with obvious
        relief and packed away the penguin suit,
I hung my black concert gown in the closet and
        tried emptiness on for size instead,
        wondering how I'd live until it would be time
        to sing again.

Remembering summers earlier on whose
        freedom grew so long that I was only
        too glad to see September come,
how could my voice wait to join the transcendence?

Now it's the unwilling suspension
        of disbelief
        that's left waiting at the door.
Our world of beauty and belonging,
        moments like bright jewels strung
        together in an enveloping garment of joy, till
        evening darkness of clouds, loss of glow
        intruded,
        is now suspended
        until such time as it can safely
        resume.

Bedside Manners

Patient, lady, please
forgive my tongue.
Death is such a common word in my world
it walked in on our conversation
quite without thinking.
How graciously you let it pass
that I who meant so well
have tripped so
clumsily against your ears.
I hope not to have done
more harm than good.

Intensive Care

Your patriarch had always grown indeed
        a little sad
        to see his children depart his world,
        striking bravely off
        on their own, the waves
        leaving the shoreline
        a bit nibbled
        in their wake.

But at least, like the tide
        they went out and came back
        with sound I could hear
        and love and touch that
        I could hold.

Now they're kept
        like precious jewels
        behind glass.

Front Lines

Long day far too long away from
        any quietness
        now the room falls
        quiet outside the purring of the
        curled-up cat.

My other's drawn face softens in sleep
        at the dinner table.

War Footing

Went to the store,
the shelves were bare.
The lack of common items there
was foolishness
or so they said.
Folks do strange things
amidst mounting dead.
Disrupted food chains lie ahead?
We'd best stock up while we still can.
Had read this road map long ago,
collecting tales of dystopian woe
in leisure reading, never
thinking it would show up for real.
Never thought what was called "tin foil" that we
washed with the dinner dishes and left to dry
in the drainer or worse, dried with towels, would
echo forward through the ages to resonate with
what's now well into a third year
sequestered awash in fear.
The germ of thought had been planted there
to simply prepare,
the scouts' motto, but living it long
is something else.

Line in the Sand

Southern lady
fire and ice, softness
and steel,
your great-grandmother grew old in an empty bed
and generations of genteel spinsters knew
who the real losers were
at Shiloh.

Beneath your crinoline manner lies
a bitter will for survival that
drove you to drive your aged mother
two thousand miles cross-country
to my vaccine clinic.
The grapevine had said we have spare doses
on hand when none could be had where
you live
for her priority age group.

Glad you called ahead.
It's in the cooler with her name on it.

Neanderthal

We were a patient people……
pardon me, a patient hominin.
Many hundred thousand years we lived
small in numbers, mostly in peace, coping with the cold
just fine.
We knew and loved beauty, like you do, created it
ourselves, mourned our dead and sought for them
a safe passage.
We made progress, innovations;
everyone always wants to leave their stamp
on the world.
Loutish beetle-browed brutes?
Not so much.
Took you 52,000 years to figure that one out.
So our Y chromosome vanished, the male one,
but not the female one
and not the autosomes either.
Outcompeted?
Discouraged into oblivion?
You think?
You took our women.
You took them by force, figuring they were
there for the taking
in a four-letter word.
Down the march of history our nucleotides
have dispersed among the new ones.
And now the domain of the disinherited
strikes back.

Compline

Now I lay me down to bed
with nine wraiths circling round my head.
The bones of hope gleam white and spare,
a saints' communion without prayer
beneath a blasted desert tree
whence that dark lady waits for me.
Bewildered faces brush my hand;
my fingers, clutching, close on sand.
Pray their love my resolve shall take
if I should cry before they wake.

Consequences

One time the time lines hung in space
poised and convergent
for how brief a passage till the
solar wind blew softly past
and drew back the curtain
on chaos.

Shaken awake by the snake curled,
hissing, around the trunk
while grownups whispered a melisma
on the market price of apples
with grave faces.

So too each subsequent new
ecological niche,
bright link in the chain of being, gains
again the resonance with overtones
unheard in the hermit's cell.

The Garden gate stands ajar upon
a finite road
where sine waves pass in graceful arches
echoing in antiphon
the Lachrymae Pavanne.

Merge

Out of the tunnel

blinking in sudden sunlight

waiting for the next

CovEncore

Thought I'd just fold and steal away, did we?
Had no appreciation for my skills in
shape-shifting then?
You do now.
The Greek alphabet certainly imparts
a touch of class I had not expected, it's just
what my kind do
well.
Keep on with your iterations, there.
I'll see that and raise you
a spike.

Protagonists

Common Demon

Do you my friend
lie too within warm but sleepless covers mulling
amidst swirling words till jumbled
thoughts coalesce and drive you shivering to fumble
for a robe and shuffle (softly so as not
to wake your sleeping other) on your darkened
desk for paper and pen to write it
all down before it's gone?

Hengest

We came in three ships the first time,
their prows cutting the water like silent knives,
and strangled these soft poets in their places.
But yet have they left us as changelings ourselves,
that we set side by side in the evening firelight the ax
and the harp.

Charismatic

Beneath the warmth and charm lies
    the invisible protective shield,
    the one-way mirror.
The constant din of voices bounces off its
    polished surface.
Tactfully it fends off the unceasing
    hordes of outstretched arms,
pleading silently
please don't
come too close.
I must
save some of myself for me, you see.

Behind the Counter

Why can't they speak up beforehand
instead of shouting after?
Crabbing and fussing is hard enough
to bear when you can hear it but
did you ever try to read the lips
of a Russian Jew?
I admit the guilt of gladness seeing
those few who know and open their
mouths wide and speak slowly.
I serve them out of turn when I can,
shrugging off your harping.
My day thus redeemed, I shall not ask
for absolution.

Duplex

Downstairs
the TV blares
her temper flares
at the world outside that can't make
    sense of her incoherent ramblings
    and illiterate scrawl.
Clang! goes the dishpan
Slam! goes the door
Crash! goes the kitchen chair
    down to the floor.
All alone
she cradles the phone
in her huge hand, grown
accustomed to holding it for hours
    on end, alternately laughing and crying
    over the lines to those who keep their distance.
Upstairs
a lover and his lady live with slippered footsteps
padding softly but for boards here and there
    that squeak,
and speak to one another
gently across the distance between
    two noses,
making no sound louder than the brass
    belt buckle falling to the
    floor with an anticipative
    clunk.

Duality

Soundless smiles and nameless joys
        find form and substance
        in our talking, taking
shape beneath our joined thoughts as though
        molded by two
        sculptors' hands as
        we kindred two are one in
        this shared universe.

Soul Mate

Your smile nestles in my
        mind like a secret
        in a pocket
Like yesterday's agates
        and centimes and beads
        and seeds
        and other tangible treasures
Kept where I can feel its
        warmth and sense
        its solid comfort.

Transmission Lines

The day's work flows its
        way through my thoughts
        and fingers, but now
        and then my mind's eye
pauses to catch a glimpse of
        you and reaches across the
        bounds of space
        to touch you.

October

Whereas your standard angular geometric display of
chrome with bright harsh blades is indeed the
appropriate form of home heat in a modern setting,
it would be adverse here where
so many years have settled in.

Our radiators stand in the corners silent
servants shoulder high coiled
in genteel oldness.
Though painted in most cases to
match their surroundings they cast on each
room an atmosphere of softness
born of having listened in on whispers and laughter
for so long.

The souls of discretion, they woke us this morning not
with sound but with unobtrusive
warmth to the touch saying
the seasons' circle has
turned another cog again.

Carmina Ohana

Raise the flagons, companions, we raise
our voices in virelais
whose keys no one can find.
The quality of our melody
peaks and then falls in a Gaussian
curve per quantity of wine consumed per
person born into an ill-fitting century,
Rapunzel crowned with man-made braids
singing from the tower window the lament
on the death of Richard the Lion-Hearted.

Table Mannerisms

The cat's crestfallen snow-white face
framed by a dark oak floor looks up
in motionless confusion.
Himself the epitome of
politeness he'd noted the
termination of your breakfast and was making
his customary approach toward your
lap when you pushed back your chair
and walked away!

Colonnade

I weep to see you

so small through your eyes, you being

so tall through mine

Grandfather

He kissed his wife and babies goodbye and left
on the train for Samarkand,
unknowing till the moment of
appointment.

Years later, we who never knew him giggled
at the love letters we found in the attic
of her house:
"My Dearest Flora, life without you
Is dark and dank----"

We always envisioned him as
Teddy Roosevelt, not being close to any
sorrows ourselves yet, waiting till
growing up to carry out of the attic into
sharpened awareness two things:

One brown lock of Grandmother's hair, silken
to the touch and three feet long;
and the story of how she took her
grief to the basement cellar, weeping in
darkness that her children
should not see her.

Guitarist I

Like lover and loved
his arms enfold the gleaming rosewood curves,
lithe fingers drawing
now a whisper
now a cry from the stroked strings
player and played blending into
one soul.

Guitarist II

Too tense this night.
> The strings bark and whine
> taut beneath stumbling fingers
> wandering away behind
> a disobedient mind
> and even her sewing thread keeps
> tangling in time to the
> snap of hickory sparks.

No refuge, the world's made too many
> synapses with the inner sanctum.

For so long have we been expecting
> an equilibrium, some arrival
> at a steady state,
> the series of hurdles so ingrained that we
> have rehearsed the colossal sigh of relief
> actually thinking we'd use it.

The realization grows we'd best not
> hold our breath for the proper occasion.

Still stumbling through the
> basement at Knossos with only
> ephemeral light in sight,
> the grazing herd has scattered into
> all turns of the tunnel
> for the vaulting.

Time Capture

Perpetual motion frozen for one instant
red rover, red rover, oh who can come over
pink lemonade pulled down onto
black and white from the crickets' buzz resounding
in sunlight against whitewashed church siding
floating on a swell of green lawn.

We were coaxed into line for our
picture with spindly knees sprouting
from shorts or under
dresses tied in bows and sashes.

A stranger's face hanging back among the rest
in the back row wrapped
in a tattered print silk scarf knotted to
one side on a small shoulder the magic
cloak of invisibility the magic carpet of
transport to elsewhere
even then the dreamer
The Gypsy Queen.

Hoople, North Dakota

The people
from Hoople
can never live it down,
the snickers
the sly winks
the evanescent frown.
How little
they all know;
they'll never even try
to journey out to Hoople
where prairie melds with sky.
Lush grass grows in communion
with salt-washed whitened scars
and roads that stretch forever
devoid of passing cars.
The silence
would scare them.
The crickets' dreaming cry
is best left
to lonely
silent watchers such as I.

Harlequin

I'm a battery of stumbling drums
a herd of ill-tuned tympani
my feet measure out their wooden tread
underneath a cross of trembling strings

My wits lose their way on the trip past my teeth
bright words lost in a murmuring sea
I stand rooted to the spot, my tongue glued tight
while the pantomime goes on unrealized still

Sometimes in a quirk the scarf's thrown off my cage
and I sing a clear tune for a stanza or two
then my spring winds down to fall silent again
Who knows who looks out from behind these bars?

Protagonists

Faces and voices
crowd forward asking speak
for me remember me
abide with me
too fast the tide flows by and only
impermanence can be counted on.

Here we have one who signs in
at the trailhead and sets out swinging
between faith and despair,
and again one who shouts down disorder
with all good intent and varying success.
These two writhe at the uprooting.
This one has survived it after a fashion,
another not, broken by the unanticipated
crumbling of symbiosis.
That one's world has capsized
Where is its anchor now?

Trapped by the cosmos's gathering chaos we stand
in the coil of the spiral arm.
Grounded in sheer obstinacy we endure
in the face of the Second Law's
inevitable triumph,
pausing in defiance
at this station of the Cross.

Antagonists

Wolf Moon

Good evening, your Excellence.
We meet again after all those
years of constant
companionship,
your shadow gracing our table,
your voice at the door, night
and day.
The inner vision of hollow
eyes and sunken cheeks, the footsteps
of fear circling us endlessly
in the snow,
were your legacy for
growing up thin inside.
Joking that our lot were always
cold
was not to laugh, but a tacit
nod to your presence
on the path going forward,
waiting behind every tree
to say, Ah
let us prey.

Ghosts

Ladies in white drifted in silent
>flocks up and down my plane of vision
>focused upon tomorrow until
>a knowing voice noted I was not
>nice enough to wear the mark,
>the cap of service.

Somehow that got translated into servitude.
The martyr's crown never did fit me very well, always
>slipping down over one ear
>where its metallic properties transmit
>all the more keenly through my skull
>the harsh clang
>of censure.

Citadel

Walls of ivy, leaves of three,
How shall we consider thee?
A hopeful beacon burning bright
by scholars' seeking day and night
to implement the healers' charge
midst buildings tall
and egos large.

Recipient

Stretched out on the gurney raised up
on one elbow his small face breaks into
a smile in chatting with a nurse
before the swinging doors of future promise.
Too excited to be drowsy he waits
awake in the hallway.

Awhile ago he feigned sleep, being
supposedly sufficiently sedated he nonetheless
opened one unobtrusive eye as the
organ perfusion machine
went by in the escort of
gowned and hooded servants,
the Ark of the Covenant,
a stranger's last gift.

He thinks, now I will be
free.

Semaphoria

How long have I lived in this house
        walking its clean hushed corridors and
        watching its catechism recited
        as a novice standing
        fascinated
        reveling in the beauty of
        Leviathan
        not truly sensing the touch
        of the tentacles
        that gathered me to
        its maw.

Ex Cathedra

The learned doctors of
varied stripes convened as seats and aisles and stairs
climbed steeply toward the stars,
gradually filling the auditorium with persons
with lunches.

Today's scholarly menu huddled at
center stage, knots of anguished parents, a
bewildered young mother holding her small
bundle of overturned hopes out for
perusal.

The drawn face of a woman facing
Round 2 and decision met that of the
smooth chief of service with slicked-back hair and
soothing voice of authority.
"It's not so bad. It's not so bad," he pronounced.

She stared at him straight and said
"You're -----
telling me -----
it's not so bad?"

Soft Money

An enterprise said to the government:
"People, we exist
here to create all that is
evolving truth and noble
knowledge for all good.

However,
you're the outfit that underwrote this empire
in our midst, our space, using our people,
in the first place.

These folks' work matches our job
description, we recruit for it, but it's
 your work they're doing, after all.

What we're providing here is, well,
a brand,
the loftiness, the cachet, of our names,
the sharing of a lighted marquee.

Therefore, *you* pay the bills, every
one, the staff of these
folks' lives."

"Well," replied the government,
"…….. okay.
Sure."

Bedeviled

With wide dark eyes she sits
in silence hounded
by furies unseen
by others,
seeing in ordinary others, enemies,
her unshared hell a black
cocoon emanating both
the waves of hate to lash
forth and the undertow sucking all
unwary into the
null point.

Stand-In

The man of my house
is gone for a while, his shoes
now filled by one whose
own stand newly bronzed upon
the fireplace mantel.

Suffer Not

The only joy that I can see
        would be in the naming.

How many possibilities
        graceful and
        uncommon,
leading the environment a bit
        beyond the end of its own nose,
        instilling a little music
        modal and extraordinary
        into the collective ear.

How important for one to be
        memorable to the world.

But at what price of peace?

46XX

I am the goddess of evil it was
    named after me the source of all
    man's sorrow
    no mention made of the possibility of
    stupidity in having seen that
    apple too and said
    yes, let's
    no momentary slip in judgement there.

The antidote's clear
    and bright as the halo pure
    and unviolated, no nicked circles here
    no base metals underlying the
    figurines, no life, no breath in the
    waxen creche,
    the essence of all that's good and true no
    deviation
    from the dance of the apes.

Prospectus

Earth mother lies in wait
dormant
asking only to be asked to
swell me like a grotesque votive
dug from a riverbed grave of eons past
A blasphemy in stone
of Titian's beauties
The vehicle of Ceres setting
the fruits of harvest to be left behind
a dried-up stalk.

Freak Show

Spectators, do you find me always
        thus noticeable or only
        when you probe?

You expect that I look with yearning on squirming smallness,
        not with distaste.

You expect that I turn away lest I weep
        with longing, not lest I weep with
        anger that you will
        not let me be,
        that you cannot ask in unconcern after
        numbers but push regret or apology
        into my answer,

and always add the epilogue, the
        raised eyebrow (too busy, I see),
        the awkward laugh when you've
        flushed out my feeling from its
        hiding place.

You may as well pelt
        me with stones or touch a
        match to me, it's
        been done before.

Praise Ye

Clap your hands ye born again
        all people far too filled with
        holiness to comprehend the Holy.
        Stamp your feet and shout
        in tongues of fire drown out
        the silence.
        Paint it a face, pluck at its sleeve,
        address it brashly standing side
        by side in unison with elbows locked against
        Otherness.

Sunrise Service

The son rose at six today or so
        they say how grateful I
        wretch should be that such
        a favor was done for me
        you could have saved yourself
        the trouble of saving me for
        whom or what I know not
        I have not asked for this golden chain
        with a noose at the end.

Wiring Diagram

A bunch of battered lines jotted on
        a million scraps of paper in piles plus
        a host of treasured topic files,
        all lined up labeled
        along a bedside corridor
        to accommodate visual cueing.

A few too many plants but can't fault those
        bite-sized tomato delights.

A few fragments of haute couture
        unrealized in the trunk.

All too many well-meant nudges
        on the road to becoming.

Wolf Eyes

There are those who swear

fealty never having felt

the teeth and the claws

they crow in exultation.

Their time too will come.

Border Lines

Jocasta

I am the root,
the unknown constant
bracketing all existence with the
power of a voice crying out
for encirclement.

My compass is not restricted
to wakes and injuries, the integral hunger
fills all dimensions and spills out
toward the nearest point source.

The fool's equation breaks into
intricate partials.

Sorting out solid geometries only
misses the point.

Dropping an unnamed term means not seeing
absence expand into raging infinity.

Border Patrol

Our precious Caliban does not
        come when called anymore.
        That which we cultivated in such
        unyielding devotion has now
        turned on us.
        How is obedience such a price
        for the gift of life?
We have set his little feet on
        the path of righteousness and he but stirs up
        the dust in defiance.
        We speak to him in reasoned tones of
        that which is done
        and he but pipes his dissonances screaming
        into our ears,
and we can but bewail
        the ledger unbalanced.

Border Crossing

Now shall thine Ariel spread his shining wings.
They've been flight-tested some and proven true;
a final pebble tossed into the springs
from which welled up what felt like love to you.
A set of rippling sad concentric rings
has blurred my face in your distorted view.
Self-pitying waves wash vainly on the shore;
no battered soul now waits there with bowed head.
To make me what you thought you'd made me for,
my heart's been set upon and left for dead
too many times—what's left is nothing more
than grieving silence, all that can's been said.
So tarry then and take the Fool with thee;
I can do nothing more than set you free.

Coda

Offertory

My single gift to give is but
        midnight madness.

I watch the world in silence
        in the sunlight, I ponder people and
        power, motives and histories,
        acquiring images
unmindful of how the mind's reel
        is constantly turning
        until it comes uncalled and
        plays back.

Words and faces and voices loom over me
        like the moon calling out the neighbors' hounds.
My incisive commentaries seem
        sometimes little better than canine chorales
        in the harsh cold light of day.

Nonetheless I give them to you for they
        contain my soul.

Standfast

Occasional poets, shall we despair
        of the scornful undertones in our name or shall we
        wear the epithet with pride knowing
        we wear the same set of chains as our more
        respectable colleagues without
        the concurrent requirement
        of malnutrition?

Séance

One needs keep the ghosts
        manageable.
Let those speak who can with ease
        in voices rippling over
        the stream bed stones,
proxies for others
who only whisper.

Mirrored Drives

Our own ghosts quarrel
as we stand by, bewildered
referees from a parallel
time continuum,
hearing different voices
sounding the same as
heard before,
whether true or not, they
never go away.

AfterImage

Can't say
why harsh words stay
with one so long
why they resurface to
nag again far beyond
the putative healing.
Has the mind some special
affinity for pain
a unique attachment from which it
is less easily displaced
than its competitors?

Poets and Other Crazy People

Poets and other crazy people stand accused
        by the mind-management business of taking
        themselves
        far too seriously as the wellspring
        of all their grief and are assured they
        must learn to laugh at themselves.

But if our gift must be a vision born of pain
        would laughter kill that too
        and leave us with nothing?

Territory

Somehow my cave of being's *still* one walled in sterile
white and chrome, floored in cold gray tiles their outlines
blurred and shifting in a crazed dance
beyond my paper and pen
held at a four-inch focal length.

I've crept in here so's not to
jar another's more peaceful pursuit,
misplaced my glasses and plunged
nose-first into a closed door in the darkness.

Now huddled shivering as before
the primeval fire built to keep open
the eye of night in the hour
when breath can scarce
cloud the mirror.

Circus Circadius

My other having lost all
      sleepiness reads the funnies on his phone, girding
      for the coming day,
while I, who give the lie
      to civilization's notion that a good
      night's sleep is a prerequisite
      to survival,
      know that the sweetest sleep comes
      with the morning sun.

Retrospective

Year fifty-two dawns

each day with joy and solace

walking hand in hand.

IndigeDaughter

Turns out, I am geared for survival

My body meets harsh conditions eye to eye
toe to toe
and backs them off

It's the soft scenarios spell trouble

An embarrassment of riches grows me too much

In the land of milk and honey my mind turns to mead
and seeks more

But try to steal my life and my blood and sooner or later
you'll strike a vein of iron

When the going gets
tough the tough get wise, wrapping
up in ancient roots
whose braided rivers create
braided songs I sing
outwitting my tormentors' ploys

Answering their taunts
"How ARE you?"

I say

"I'm here"

Standoff

The ground of being
        and I have stared across the
        unbreachable chasm
        to conclude a settlement
        liveable, barely, an
        understanding that we
        leave each other alone.

Spectrescopy

Arachne's web stands
bare and dry stretched between
two blades of grass its
arid strands can hold
no more tears in the sunlit morning.
What grace was there is
gone and blessed are the wary
who will fly past without
fanning any breeze.
She gropes her way to
the corner of creation waiting
in blind hunger.

Lost Wax

I needed to be molded
sculpted
re-formed
into something—
not someone, something
acceptable
which was not the case here.

The tools were
commonplace,
mostly words instead of
sticks but also
confiscation of that which was
precious
to me,
leaving me bereft
of agency.

Well, as befits the casting process there was
 a burn as well.

Small wonder that every embarkation on
a new life found me
face to face
with the old one.

Reframed

Such are the changing fortunes of a word, that
    selfish has lost its tail and gained a new respect,
    self-directed being not a term that
    screams at one who can only live in what
    may be, granted, a private hell but
    at least it feels like home.

Cædmon, sing mē

Let me but raise my voice
        however small
unto an empty heaven and
        a distant no one
it will nonetheless
        be joyful
for you have given me back
a long-lost wholeness
wherein my voice cannot wait to join the massed
sound rising tier by tier until all feeling
hangs suspended and motionless
outside of time.

Acknowledgments

Thanks to many more than can be named:

First and foremost, my Jacques for pride, encouragement, and persistent nudging.

The Hawaii Writers Guild for the impetus and the tools to move off the dime.

A wise counselor or few.

Ohana (Hawaiian for family) of birth and that of choice.

Early adopters and outside primaries.

Conductors, agents, and guides on an unacclaimed Underground Railroad.

My Saami foremothers for the spirit of *sisu*: >12,000 years of being impossible.

The chorus of supporters human and feline.

Numerous hoku (stars) of choral and early music. Learn more about them through the author's web site: www.9volcanoespublishing.wordpress.com

And my Jacques for all the more that words cannot say.

Selected Explanations

Survivors, Hengest, and October were published in *The Gorge Literary Journal*, The Hood River News 2018-2020.

These poems were published in *Latitudes,* literary review of the Hawaii Writers, Guild Editions 1-3, 2020-2022:

https://www.hawaiiwritersguild.com/literary-review.html

46XX (1); Covirion, Consequences, and Neanderthal (2); Wolf Moon, Border Patrol, and Border Crossing (3).

Front Matter

A recent Internet article by a travel writer waxed enthusiastic about strong points of tourist travel to Hawaii, including the facts that it uses the American dollar for its currency and most of its inhabitants speak English. Note that Hawaii actually became the 50th state of the American union in 1959.

Observational Studies

US Death Toll of Mass Casualty Events 1860-mid 2022

US Civil War	750,000
World War I	117,000
1918 Influenza Pandemic	675,000
World War II	418,500
Covid-19 Pandemic	>1,000,000 to date

Neanderthal

Paleoanthropologist Dr. Erik Trinkhaus first suggested that Neanderthals had interbred with early modern humans after observing hybrid skeletal features. Ancient DNA sequencing pioneered by Dr. Svante Pääbo showed that many people carry a small percentage of Neanderthal DNA, different Neanderthal genes in different people, so that overall 40% of the Neanderthal genome is distributed across the genome of modern humans. Dr. Pääbo humorously noted that some men wrote to him that they were certain that they were Neanderthals ...... and many more women wrote to him that they were certain their *husbands* were Neanderthals. In October 2022 Dr. Pääbo was awarded the Nobel Prize in Physiology or Medicine for his signal achievements.

Severe Covid leaves its victims breathless, succumbing to a systemic failure called "cytokine storm." Genetic association studies by Drs. Pääbo and Zeberg found a specific snippet of DNA on chromosome 3, termed 3p21.31, that is responsible for increased disease severity and fatalities when it is present in Covid patients carrying the Neanderthal version of the snippet instead of the modern human version. This particular segment of DNA had interbred from Neanderthals into modern humans ~ 60,000 years ago. Subsequent studies by Downes *et al* showed that the severe disease outcome was due to hyperactivity of a particular gene called LZTFL1.

Zeberg, H. and Pääbo, S. The major genetic risk factor for severe COVID-19 is inherited from Neanderthals. *Nature* **587**, 610–612 (2020)

Downes, D.J., Cross, A.R., Hua, P. *et al.* Identification of *LZTFL1* as a candidate effector gene at a COVID-19 risk locus. *Nat Genet* **53,** 1606–1615 (2021). https://doi.org/10.1038/s41588-021-00955-3

Protagonists

Grandfather

My grandfather was a railroad locomotive engineer. His train route took him through a railroad crossing in urban Minneapolis just a few blocks from his family's home. My grandmother would pack up the 5 kids and they'd all stand at the crossing to exchange waves with him as he drove his steam engine by. One day in January 1930, due to negligent maintenance by the railroad company, the steam engine exploded in mid-trip in an isolated area where rescue amid sub-zero conditions was long delayed. Critically burned, he was initially cited in the news media as expected to recover; my grandmother took an hours-long train trip daily to visit him in the hospital for 3 weeks until he died. Subsequent decades of biomedical research into trauma have shown that this combination of major injury/burns and delay in treatment pushes the body into the same fatal program of systemic failure as that caused by Covid: cytokine storm.

Hoople N.D.

The father of a family friend where I grew up was from Hoople. Wikipedia cites Hoople as a city in Walsch County, North Dakota, population 247 in the 2020 census, founded in 1889. The town's other renown is Peter

Schickele, professor in the Extension division of the Musicolology and Musical Pathology departments of the University of Southern North Dakota at Hoople, who devoted his life to bringing forward the music of PDQ Bach, oddest of Johann Sebastian Bach's 20-odd children.

Antagonists

Recipient

Human solid organ transplantation has saved many lives, from kidney to heart and liver transplants, encouraged by permission for organ donation on drivers' licenses. Many still remain on waiting lists for organ transplants.

Soft Money

A man said to the universe:
"Sir I exist!"
"However," replied the universe,
"The fact has not created in me
A sense of obligation."

Poem by Stephen Crane (1871-1900) from *War Is Kind* (1899)

Multiple Poems

See: *A Stranger Asked Me If I Felt Like 'Less Of A Woman' Because I Don't Have Children*

https://www.huffpost.com/entry/woman-in-40s-no-kids-childfree_n_63116048e4b0aefceeca1e5a
by Louise Slyth (9/5/2022)

Border Lines

Borderline Personality Disorder, cited in the Diagnostic and Statistical Manual of Mental Disorders (DSM-5) , is a complex psychiatric condition of emotional dysregulation that displays pathologic fear of abandonment and misperception of neutral interpersonal interactions as hostile. Its underlying mechanisms remain a mystery. One suggestion is aberrations in the developmental wiring of brain regions that process affiliation or abandonment and assessment of external threats. Yet another focuses on early traumatic life events. Certainly a combination of factors may also be possible. Such a pattern of ideas and actions can readily be mistaken for cultural perceptions or expectations if BPD is not recognized. In any case, this behavioral trajectory can wreak substantial collateral damage on those nearby, the "unseen casualties" who have been impacted by its influence.

Kang, S.J., Liu, S., Ye, M., Kim, D.-I., Pao, G.M., Copits, B.A., Roberts, B.Z., Lee, K.-F., Bruchas, M.R., and Han, S. **A central alarm system that gates multi-sensory innate threat cues to the amygdala.** *Cell Reports*, 2022; 40 (7) : 111222 DOI: 10.1016/j.celrep.2022.111222

Press release, Salk Institute for Biological Studies. **How the brain gathers threat cues and turns them into fear.** https://www.sciencedaily.com/releases/2022/08/220816120208.htm.

Kwon, D. **Borderline Personality Disorder May Be Rooted in Trauma.** Originally published with the title "The Long Shadow of Trauma" in Scientific American 326, 1, 48-55 (January 2022) doi:10.1038/scientificamerican0122-48

Coda

Circus Circadius

Knowing that people can be larks (morning persons) or owls (night persons) long predates our emerging knowledge about circadian rhythm biology and its molecular drivers. The latter are a set of clock proteins that tick away in each of our cells under the watchful purview of a brain master timekeeper. Entrainment of the master clock by sunlight is believed to nudge our noses to a 24-hour grindstone that in a perfect world matches the earth's rotational day/night light/dark cycle and its proxy, the daily business cycle. However, "morningness" or "eveningness" is a spectrum among individuals, based in variations among many clock genes.

We of the owl chronotypical predilection, present from birth and in multiple family members, may simply have a variant form of one or more clock genes. For example, the clock molecule Per3 is one such gene having variations that can make people more owl-like in their timing. Such a mismatch between inner hourglass and societal imperatives has come to be viewed in certain quarters as a disease (delayed sleep-wake phase disorder). Treatment aimed at reprogramming our inner clock, forcing our inherent rhythms back to the majority grindstone, rarely prevails; at the earliest opportunity we slip back into our innate time line that guarantees the most restful sleep between about 7 and 11 a.m. Sweet dreams!

Indigedaughter

Those of us whose genes hail from 70° north latitude (the Arctic Circle is at 66.5° north) are a paradigm of stubborn human survival and adaptability. Millenia lived in ~ 2 months of endless sunlight and ~ 2 months of endless night each year has selected some among us for a more prevalent ability to extract restful sleep from constant light and and function well in prolonged darkness. We've had plenty of time to learn how best to adapt our rhythms to life's demands, while also withstanding social imperatives to burn us as witches or convert us into compliant consumers and worshippers and worker bees; somehow all that just failed to obliterate us. Now, as evolving technology shapes a world endlessly bathed in artificial lighting, some of us among the Saami Diaspora join others of the owl persuasion in burning the midnight oil, providing the world with the late-shift effort it increasingly demands. There's no dichotomy between herding and coding. Just let us sleep in.

Disclaimer

To those who perceive
familiar reflections
peering from the page,
think of that tune "It ain't
necessarily so."
So then here's the Brain Teaser:
Composer? Piece? Voice?

Bookends

No accident that this poetic construct is bracketed by titles of music forms. These poems were written while thinking about, listening to, and peforming music that spans millenia of human experience and lives today. This was not a lonely experience but shared with like minds and voices in a Lady Mass of 8th century Anglo-Saxon England, shimmering Gregorian chant in parallel 4ths, haunting Renaissance polyphony, soaring amid J.S. Bach's masterpieces, to Vaugh Williams and and 21st century composers. Its story is woven through these writings.

For those new to the particular Early Music space, the Information Age stands at your service with resources to get you started via your preferred search engine or links below. Renaissance choral polyphony is a good *intrada*, in 2 videos by English group The Sixteen. I've sung both.

Warning: may be habit-forming.

Libera nos, salva nos by John Sheppard (1515-1558) evokes a time, alas recently repeated, when not everyone survived to morning. A virtual performance in May 2020 features each Sixteen singer performing individually from lockdown at home; digital tracks were then merged. This video conveys both the ethereal essence of the music and the impact of the Covid pandemic, underscoring the role of technology in mitigating isolation. Note especially director Christophers in cutoff jeans, the pet audiences, and the singer in his bubble bath wearing a shower cap.

https://www.youtube.com /watch?v=jAbAtsaApZk

At the other end of the complexity spectrum is **"Spem in Allium" by Thomas Tallis (1505-1585)** better known as "The 40-Part Motet" based on its design for eight 5-part choirs of voices singing back and forth across a resonating space. Major challenge: all voices ending simultaneously. Nicknamed "Spam in Aluminum," this iconic piece can sometimes best the best efforts of a brave choir.

https://www.youtube.com/watch?v=QmH1nZSGIyY

Answer to Brain Teaser

Composer: George Gershwin
Aria in his opera Porgy and Bess
Sung by character Sportin' Life about religion

About the Author

Nancy Lewis Baenziger Ph.D. lived a first career publishing scholarly papers as a life sciences professor whose students called her "Dr. B." Her initial discovery of a VIP (Very Important Protein) she named TSP, later claimed by other scientists who hoped nobody would notice, simply strengthened her resolve to outlast adversity. Her later discovery of a Tau protein-targeting signal corps within human cells that goes rogue in Alzheimer's Disease was scorned by other scientists who now study Tau as a centerpiece of disease pathogenesis and hope nobody notices. She formally retired with honor from academia the day before her dismissal by e-mail took effect. Reading her poetry at the Hawai'i Writers Guild, Living Arts Gallery of Hawi, and Columbia Center for the Arts in Hood River, OR, Nancy now revels in a second life as a writer and a choral music singer (Tenor II) drawn to early music (as in Hildegard of Bingen ca 1150 C.E., not as in "before Elvis"). She writes poetry, essays on health care policy, and nascent thriller novels from Hawaii Island and Oregon's Columbia Gorge, in view of 9 named volcanoes, two of whom are erupting as of publication 11-12/2022.

www.ingramcontent.com/pod-product-compliance
Lightning Source LLC
Chambersburg PA
CBHW070854050426
42453CB00012B/2197